TODAY'S WORLD

LIFE ON EARTH

LINDA GAMLIN

GLOUCESTER PRESS
London · New York · Toronto · Sydney

CONTENTS

WHAT IS LIFE?	**4**
ENERGY FOR LIFE	6
MAINTAINING LIFE	8
GROWTH AND DEVELOPMENT	10
SENSITIVITY	12
LIVING COMMUNITIES	**14**
FOOD WEBS AND PYRAMIDS	16
RELATIONSHIPS	18
POPULATIONS	20
HABITATS	**22**
CONSERVATION	28
ENDANGERED SPECIES	30
PRESERVING WILDLIFE	32
EXTINCTION CHART	**34**
GLOSSARY	**35**
INDEX	**36**

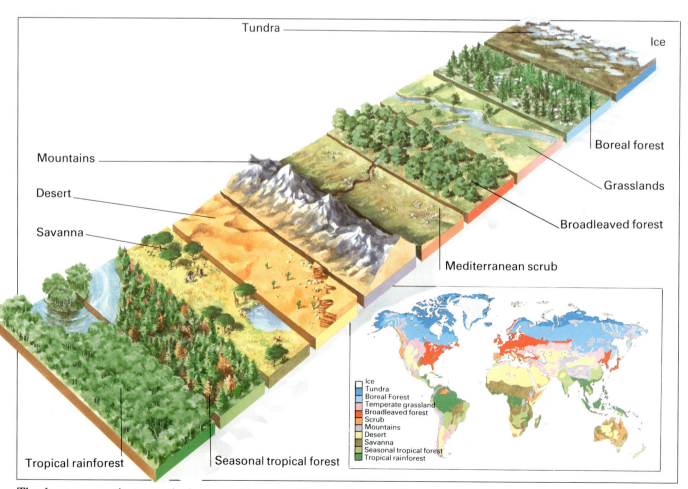

The front cover photograph shows an Emperor Gum moth caterpillar

INTRODUCTION

Every part of the Earth – from the tundra to the tropics, and mountaintop to ocean floor – is teeming with life. At any particular time, all of Earth's life forms – plants and animals – are in balance with each other and with the soil, air and water around them. But it is a delicate balance, and a change in any one factor brings about changes in others.

One of the biggest influences on the balance of nature is the activity of human beings. We are changing the environment too fast for many plants and animals to adapt to the changes. People chop down trees and the exposed soil is washed away. And because trees release oxygen into the air, it is not only the forest plants and animals that may ultimately be affected. The oxygen in the Earth's atmosphere – something that all organisms depend on – is being reduced as huge areas of forest are cleared for roads and agriculture. A greater awareness of the various factors that have led to the extinction of many species can help to save the life forms that remain.

All life on Earth has adapted to the climate and food supply.

WHAT IS LIFE?

The Earth is home to countless organisms. In temperate regions, every hectare of land (1 hectare = 2.5 acres) supports up to 300 million invertebrate animals, such as insects and worms. Together they weigh about 1,000 kg (about 1 ton). There are also about 1,700 kg (1.9 tons) of bacteria, 2,500 kg (2.8 tons) of fungi and 55 tonnes (60 tons) of plant life. Decayed plants pass back into the soil to form humus, which helps to make it fertile.

Everything in the world is either living or non-living. Living things can be divided into two groups – plants and animals. A tree or a cow is obviously living, and a rock or a handful of sand is non-living. But it is difficult to decide about some microscopic organisms. For example viruses, which cause diseases in animals and plants, are on the threshold between life and non-life. On their own they cannot grow or reproduce – they are as inactive as a crystal of sugar. But once they are inside another living cell, they can reproduce, making thousands of copies of themselves. So are viruses really alive? They probably evolved from living things, but can now exist only as parasites that depend on other cells for everything they need. The main features of all truly living things is that they have to feed to stay alive, they can grow and they can reproduce.

Structure and function

All living things have to obtain food. Most also need oxygen – from the air or from oxygen dissolved in water – and many have to move around to catch their food. All the various parts of a living body have a role to play in the difficult business of staying alive. In a typical land animal, such as a human or a cat, the digestive system takes in food and extracts from it the things it needs. The lungs take in air and extract oxygen from it. Muscles enable it to move around, and the bones of the skeleton give the muscles something to pull against. The nervous system helps to coordinate all these activities.

We can easily see many plants and animals that are around us. But there are also many living things, such as bacteria and microscopic fungi, that are so small we cannot see them. After they die, all living things can be broken down into simpler chemicals by decomposers such as bacteria and fungi. Non-living things include rocks, soil, water and man-made materials such as glass and plastic. Many man-made materials do not decompose; a bottle buried in the ground lasts for ever.

■ Living
□ Non-living

Animals

Animals eat plants or other animals as food. Six main types of animals can be seen in this picture: insects, fish, amphibians, reptiles, birds and mammals. There are also many kinds of small animals, such as worms and spiders, living in the soil, under the fallen log, in the pond and among the plants.

Plants

Plants use sunlight and photosynthesis to make food. All the major groups of plants can be seen here: flowering plants, conifers, ferns, mosses and algae. Most kinds of algae, such as pondweeds and seaweeds, live in water. Some are found in the soil or on the trunks of trees. And some are so small that they can be seen only using a microscope. Fungi are immobile like plants, but cannot use photosynthesis. Like animals they feed on other dead or dying organisms, such as the fallen tree in the picture.

Non-living things

There are many non-living things in the picture: rocks, soil, water, glass, plastic and the man-made materials of the boy's clothes. Although soil and water are not themselves alive, they provide living space for animals and plants, such as fish and the many small creatures that live under the ground.

ENERGY FOR LIFE

> In terms of weight, plants are the major living organisms on Earth – they make up 99 per cent of the world's living matter. The other 1 per cent consists of animal life, more than four-fifths of which are insects. For every human on earth, there are about 200 million insects.

All living things require energy to enable them to grow and reproduce. Animals get the energy they need from food – either plants or other animals – although some foods are richer in energy than others. Most plants are a poor source of energy and plant-eating animals (herbivores) have to eat a lot. A male African elephant has to eat 200kg (440 lb) of vegetable matter every day just to stay alive. Meat is a more concentrated source of energy, and meat-eating animals (carnivores) eat much less. By contrast, plants make most of their own food through photosynthesis (see below).

Plants and photosynthesis

The leaves of plants are green because they contain a green pigment called chlorophyll. This is contained in small round bodies called chloroplasts within the plants' leaves. Chlorophyll can absorb sunlight, which plants convert into another form of energy during photosynthesis. Here, plants use the energy of sunlight to convert water (which is sucked up through their roots) and carbon dioxide (which enters their leaves from the air) into sugars and starch, and to build tissues of cellulose. A by-product of photosynthesis is oxygen, which plants release into the air through their leaves. By making food for themselves, plants help to keep millions of other living things alive – the herbivores that eat plants and the carnivores that eat the herbivores, and everything that breathes oxygen. Dying plants are also a source of food and energy for fungi and bacteria, which in turn supply healthy plants with carbon dioxide, water and simple chemicals.

All plants, even jungle trees, depend on sunlight for life.

Herbivores

Herbivores that eat grass and leaves range in size from slugs and caterpillars to elephants and rhinoceroses. Some, such as cattle and sheep, graze on plants near the ground. Others, like giraffes and monkeys, reach up to or climb trees to get at their leaves. Animals such as many kinds of birds that feed on nuts and fruits are another type of herbivore. Some animals, including humans, eat both plants and meat – they are known as omnivores.

Cattle are domesticated herbivores.

Carnivores

Carnivores include many ferocious predators such as lions and eagles. Also in this group are scavengers such as hyenas and vultures, which feed on dead animals. But not all carnivores are like these. For instance centipedes, which live in the soil, are carnivores that eat smaller animals. Some snakes and birds specialize in eating eggs. Most bats are carnivores that prey on insects. Other insect-eaters include armadillos, anteaters and pangolins.

Lions are carnivores that hunt their prey.

Energy flow

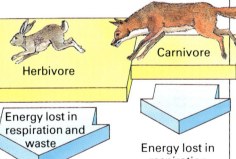

The sun's energy is absorbed by plants during photosynthesis (see opposite). But as this energy flows from one food source to another only a part of it is passed on from plants to a plant-eating herbivore. The herbivore, in turn, uses up a lot of the energy it takes in just to stay alive and active. Some energy goes toward making new cells or repairing old or injured ones. Energy is also used to power muscles that enable an animal to move and breathe and to keep its heart pumping. In young animals, energy is needed to build up new tissue as they grow. As energy is used up in growth and movement, or lost to the air as heat, there is even less passed on to a carnivore.

MAINTAINING LIFE

All living organisms need oxygen. The oxygen in the air is produced by plants. Nearly three-quarters of it comes from microscopic plant-like organisms in the phytoplankton that floats in the upper layers of the oceans. Much of the rest comes from trees in the world's forests.

In addition to energy, nearly all living things need water and air. In fact water, contained within cells and in blood and other body fluids, accounts for more than half the weight of many creatures. Living things also need nutrients. Plants get these from the soil, and they include minerals such as nitrates and phosphates. To remain healthy, animals require certain trace elements (chemical elements that are present in minute quantities), such as calcium for making bones and teeth, and iron (which is a vital constituent of blood). All these elements have to come from food.

Water and oxygen

Apart from a few types of bacteria, living things need oxygen. Land animals get it from air, which is 21 per cent oxygen (the rest is nitrogen with traces of carbon dioxide and other gases). Fish, crabs and other animals that breathe using gills absorb oxygen from water, which can dissolve up to 3 per cent of the gas.

Even in air-breathing animals, the oxygen first has to dissolve in a layer of watery fluid lining their lungs. Some of this water evaporates and is breathed out, so that in obtaining oxygen the animals tend to lose water, especially if the air is very dry. Desert animals, such as camels, have long nostrils to recapture any water vapour from the air leaving their lungs.

The leaves of plants take in air through tiny holes called stomata. They are generally on the undersides of leaves, in the shade away from sunlight, and can be closed during the daytime if necessary. In some desert plants, the stomata are tucked away in furrows or pits to reduce still further the risk of drying out.

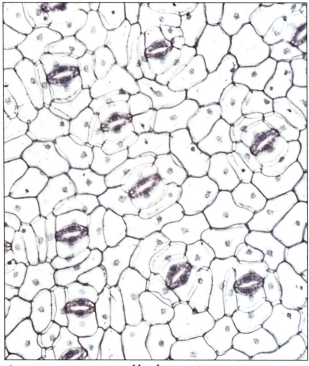
A microscopic view of leaf stomata

Camels have ways of conserving water.

Doing without the Sun

In the dark ocean depths there are communities of strange creatures that survive without sunlight. They get their energy ultimately in the form of chemically rich hot water that spews out of cracks in the Earth's crust. These hot spots on the sea bed are called hydrothermal vents. Minerals in the hot water feed bacteria, which can harness chemical energy to make food. Millions of the bacteria live in the water around the hydrothermal vents and they provide food for animals that filter the bacteria from the water, including shellfish and giant pogonophoran worms. These worms are up to 3.5m (11ft) long and 10cm (4 in) around. They have no mouths so they must absorb the bacteria through the skin of their tentacles that emerge from the tip. Other deep-sea creatures also live in permanent blackness, but they feed on smaller aquatic animals and debris that rain down from the upper layers of the water.

Giant pogonophoran worms on the sea bed

Body-building

When plants photosynthesize they use water from the soil and carbon dioxide from the air to make a simple sugar called glucose. Photosynthesis takes place in the leaves and the glucose is carried through the plant in sap. By stringing together long chains of glucose molecules the plant makes cellulose, a tough material that forms cell walls and the structural parts of plants. Glucose can also form starch, which it uses to store food in the roots (as in potatoes) or in the seeds (as in cereals such as wheat). Plants such as beans can turn glucose into proteins, sunflowers can turn it into oils that are stored in their seeds, and apples and grapes turn it into another sugar called fructose, which makes their fruits taste sweet.

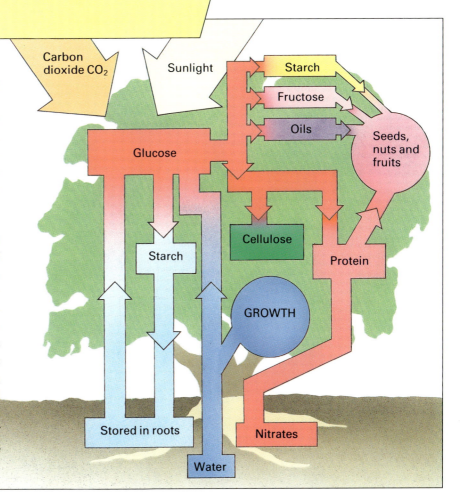

GROWTH AND DEVELOPMENT

Animals and plants are made up of cells. A large mammal such as a bull may have as many as a million million cells in its body. Each animal cell is only about .015 of a millimetre across. Most plant cells are three times as big, but bacteria are only .002 of a millimetre.

Almost all living things are made up of cells. Cells are tiny packets of living matter that can stack together, like building blocks, to form tissues and organs. Each cell has a thin outer skin, or membrane, enclosing a mass of jelly-like protoplasm, which consists mostly of water and protein.

All life processes take place within cells – including the breakdown of food for energy, and the building up of materials to make new cells. Unlike animal cells, the cells of plants have rigid walls made of cellulose (see below), which provide support.

New cells

At the heart of animal and plant cells is a round body called the nucleus. Inside this are chromosomes, which contain DNA, the chemical that carries all the information needed to build a cell. By "reading" the information in the DNA, the cell can assemble the materials for making a new cell like itself. Once it has grown large enough, it divides to give two new cells. At the same time the cell makes a copy of its DNA, so that when it divides, each new cell is carrying the same information. This is an important difference between living and non-living things: a grain of sand cannot produce another grain of sand.

Animal and plant cells are not exactly the same. Most animal cells have flexible membranes, whereas cell walls of plants are rigid and made of cellulose. When a plant cell divides, the two new cells are separated at first by a membrane. Then special chemical processes in the cytoplasm (the part of the protoplasm surrounding the nucleus) produce cellulose. It is added to the membrane to create a new cell wall.

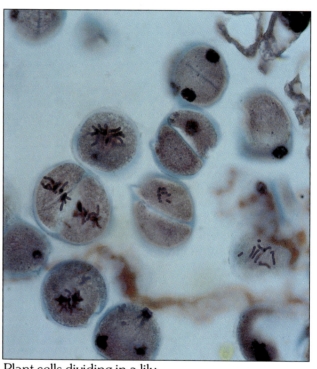

Plant cells dividing in a lily

A dividing plant cell has no vacuoles (storage spaces) and a large nucleus.

The nucleus divides first. A new cell wall develops.

The cytoplasm adds layers of cellulose to each side of the new cell wall.

The newly formed vacuoles join together. These will later form also in the smaller cell.

From egg to embryo

Adult plants and animals may contain billions of cells, but they all start life as a single cell, the fertilized egg (1). This cell divides repeatedly to make all the cells in the adult. At each division the cell splits in two, so the numbers build up only slowly at first (2). After the first division there are two cells, then four, then eight. The numbers then increase more quickly – 16, 32, 64, 128, and so on.

By the time the embryo of an animal gets to this stage, it forms a hollow ball of cells called a blastula (3). The ball then collapses on itself, like a squashed tennis ball, at the gastrula stage. The cells on the outside of the gastrula are destined to become the skin of the animal, and those on the inside will become its stomach and intestines. As the cells continue to divide, the embryo elongates and the individual organs begin to form (4).

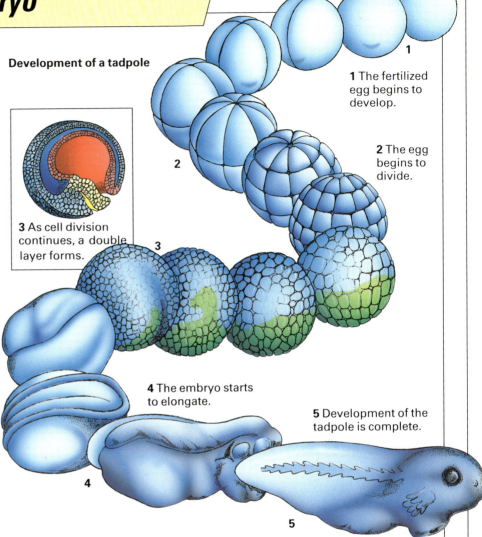

Development of a tadpole

1 The fertilized egg begins to develop.

2 The egg begins to divide.

3 As cell division continues, a double layer forms.

4 The embryo starts to elongate.

5 Development of the tadpole is complete.

Getting bigger

Animals that have skeletons to support their bodies have special problems when they grow larger, because the skeleton must get bigger too. Young mammals have growing areas near the ends of the bones. There the cells have not yet become hardened with minerals, so they can keep dividing. Animals such as insects and crustaceans (like crabs and lobsters) have their skeletons are on the outsides of their bodies – they have exoskeletons. They grow as much as they can inside them, and then find a safe place to moult. The exoskeleton splits open, and the animal struggles free. It has formed a new exoskeleton inside the old one and, before it hardens, the animal pumps itself up with air or water to make the new skeleton bigger.

Insects moult when they outgrow their exoskeletons.

SENSITIVITY

Many animals have special senses. Migrating birds, for example, can detect the length of the day. They do not do this with their eyes, but with a mysterious part of the brain called the pineal gland or "third eye". It responds to light passing through the bones of the skull.

For most animals, survival depends on having good information about the world around them. They get this information from sense organs, such as a nose, eyes and ears. Humans are sensitive to several different things: light, sound, heat, cold, touch and certain chemicals (through the senses of taste and smell). Some animals can respond to other things we are unaware of, such as magnetism (which helps birds to navigate), electric fields (which help some fish find prey buried in the mud of the sea bed) or even the length of the day.

Plant responses

Plants need light in order to survive, and their response to it is very strong. A houseplant turned away from a window bends back towards the light within a few days. This happens because the light falling on the tip of the stem stimulates it to produce a hormone. The hormone gradually trickles down through the cells on the side of the stem where it is produced – the side nearest the light. It slows down growth, but the cells on the other, darker side of the stem continue to grow at the normal rate. As a result, the stem gradually bends towards the light, and once this happens hormone production stops.

Plants also detect gravity, and send their roots downwards in response to it. Some plants have other senses as well, to suit their special ways of life. The ivy-leaved toadflax, for example, is a plant that grows on rocky cliffs and walls. As its seed-pods ripen they respond to light by growing away from it. They place their ripe seeds into dark cracks in the rock or wall – the best place for them to germinate and grow.

Most plants grow towards the light.

The toadflax grows towards the dark.

Clocks and rhythms

Although we may not be aware of it, like most animals and plants we have a built-in "biological clock". In humans, it slows down our bodies in the evening and gets them going again in the morning. But copepods which feed on plankton in the sea have a biological clock that tells them to rise to the surface to feed at night, then to swim down deeper and rest during the day.

Another type of biological clock tells plants and animals what season of the year it is, so that birds know when to start courting and building nests and plants know when to come into flower. They "measure" the length of the daylight hours every day, and when the day reaches a particular length they know it must be spring.

Crowned cranes displaying while courting

Phytoplankton
Copepod
Mid-day   Midnight   Mid-day

Scents and smells

Chemical senses – taste and smell – are very useful for finding food. Butterflies find flowers by their scent, and sharks can follow the smell of blood in the water to locate an injured fish. Scents are also useful for communication. Some female moths emit special chemicals called pheromones to attract male moths. The males have scent detectors on their huge feathery antennae. Male deer produce scent from special glands to mark their territories and warn off rivals.

Male Atlas moths have scent detectors.

A roe deer marks its territory using scent.

LIVING COMMUNITIES

Many plants rely on animals for pollination and seed dispersal, just as animals need plants for food and shelter. Scientists estimate that whenever a species of plant becomes extinct, about 30 animals – mostly small invertebrates – also become extinct because, directly or indirectly, their lives depended on that plant.

In 1982, a biologist working in a tropical forest found 600 new insect species in just one type of tree.

All living systems are the product of evolution, a very slow and probably gradual process of change that can produce new species of all kinds of organisms – both plant and animal. Evolution is going on all the time, but too slowly for us to notice it. In a living community, any change in one species affects many others, because their lives are all interlinked. So relationships that exist today are the result of a long process of evolving together.

Eventually, this kind of coevolution can lead to specialists, such as the yucca moth and the yucca weevil, with only one food source. Or it can produce generalists, like the cactus wren, able to eat a wide range of foods. When there is a sudden change in the climate, specialists suffer badly; if the yucca trees die out so will the yucca moth. Generalists tend to evolve into new species adapted to the new conditions.

Living systems

Biologists divide the natural world into smaller units they can study. The smallest unit is an individual organism. It belongs to a population – all the members of that species living within the area. The species also forms part of a community – all the different organisms in the area. The next level is the ecosystem, which includes the community as well as the soil, water and other non-living features. Biologists also try to identify the different types of organisms in an ecosystem – herbivores, carnivores and decomposers. They aim to work out how they interact today, and how they have evolved together to produce the present ecosystem. They recognize many distinctive types of ecosystems and call these biomes. Broadleaved woodland is just one type; others include desert, coral reef and tropical rainforest.

INDIVIDUAL (ladybird)

POPULATION (ladybirds)

COMMUNITY (plants, ladybirds, caterpillars, aphids, ants, birds)

ECOSYSTEM (Soil, plants, plant-eaters, meat-eaters, decomposers)

BIOME (broadleaved woodland)

YUCCA TREE

A typical community from the American Mojave Desert. The yucca feeds herbivores, such as the yucca moth, weevils, tortoises and rabbits. The insects are food for carnivores such as the elf owl, cactus wren and lizards. These in turn may feed other carnivores, such as snakes.

Cactus wren
This large wren feeds on grasshoppers, beetles, ants and small lizards that live around the base of desert plants. It often makes its nest in a yucca, and sings from its topmost branches.

Elf owl
This tiny, sparrow-sized owl feeds on insects, catching them in flight. It often nests in holes in cacti and other desert plants – the holes are made by woodpeckers.

Yucca moth
This small moth depends totally on the yucca, and the yucca relies on the moth to pollinate its flowers. The adult moth takes balls of pollen from one flower to another and lays its eggs in it. The moth's caterpillars feed on yucca seeds.

Weevil
This insect feeds on the tissues of the yucca. The female uses its long snout to bore into the plant, and lays its eggs in the hole. When the larvae hatch they are surrounded by food.

Rabbit
A race of cottontail rabbit has evolved in the desert. It does not have to drink water, but can get all the moisture it needs from plants.

Soil
Many small animals such as worms, insects and spiders live, feed and lay eggs in the soil.

Snake
Desert snakes have thick waterproof skins to conserve moisture. They can survive long periods without food, then eat one large meal when they get the chance.

Termites
A dead yucca provides food for termites, which feed on such waste materials, decompose them, and return them to the soil.

Tortoise
Like the rabbit, the desert tortoise eats plants. But instead of running away from its enemies, it hides in its shell, which also prevents it from losing moisture.

15

FOOD WEBS AND PYRAMIDS

The Earth's plants produce 133 billion tonnes of new material every year, 33 per cent of it in forests. In spite of this production, the total weight of plants on Earth does not increase. Indeed the total weight of all living things on the planet – called the biomass – is fairly constant.

One way of studying ecosystems is to look at how energy and nutrients flow through them, from one type of organism to another. The situation varies in different types of biomes. In a tropical forest, for example, there is abundant rainfall and it is warm all the year round, so plants grow very quickly. As a result there are more herbivores with an ample food supply and carnivores feeding on them than there would be in an unproductive biome such as a desert. A sequence of species that eat each other is called a food chain. Food chains that are cross-linked with each other form food webs.

Feeding systems

All animals eat to stay alive. And most animals are eaten by something else. Biologists who study such relationships (called ecologists) show them as diagrams known as food chains.

Some food chains are very short – rabbits eat grass and foxes eat rabbits is a good example. When a fox dies of disease or old age, decomposers such as bacteria and fungi break down the carcass and return the nutrients to the soil. The nutrients may help to grow more grass for rabbits to eat, but there is an important difference here: no energy is flowing back to the plants, only nutrients such as nitrates.

Some food chains are much longer than this, and most interconnect with others. For example, wolves also eat rabbits, many rabbits die of disease, and omnivores such as badgers or bears may eat baby rabbits but they also eat plants. Because food chains are interlinked in this complicated way, it is better to think in terms of a food web, drawn as a network with energy and nutrients flowing in various directions.

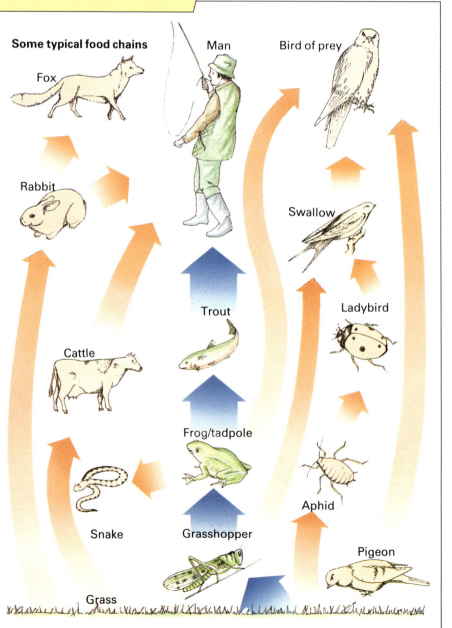

Some typical food chains

Numbers and sizes

If all the organisms in a food web were piled up in a heap they would form a huge food pyramid. The number of predators (such as foxes) is always much lower than the number of prey (the rabbits). With long food chains the numbers get smaller at each step along the chain. The animal at the end of the chain, can never be very numerous because there is simply not enough food.

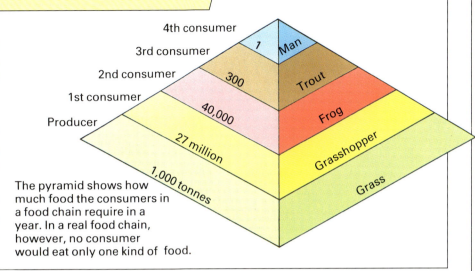

The pyramid shows how much food the consumers in a food chain require in a year. In a real food chain, however, no consumer would eat only one kind of food.

The problems of pollution

In the modern world, being a top predator has its problems. Some chemicals, such as pesticides, are not broken down by the body in the way that food is broken down. So when an animal eats such substances they stay inside its body. A carnivore feeding on that animal is eating all the accumulated chemicals as well — and passes them along to the next carnivore in the food chain. At each step in the chain, the chemicals become more and more concentrated.

The insecticide DDT, now banned in many countries, accumulates in this way. It is dangerous to all animals, including humans. But it is especially bad for birds of prey because it makes their eggshells fragile. The eggs break in the nest, so no chicks are produced.

Another pesticide, Dieldrin, affects predators such as otters because it gets into rivers, and thus into fish. Dieldrin is still used in some places, and where this happens many otters die a slow and painful death by poisoning.

Radioactive materials cannot be broken down by the body either. In northern Scandinavia, the people known as Lapps eat mainly reindeer meat. Following the nuclear accident at Chernobyl in the Soviet Union, radioactive fallout contaminated the lichens on which reindeer feed. The radioactivity became concentrated in the reindeer meat, so the Lapps could no longer safely eat it.

River pollution is a threat to otters as well as fish.

Radioactive fallout has contaminated reindeer food.

RELATIONSHIPS

Coevolution results in many interesting relationships between species. Often different plants and animals compete for the same resource. The effects of this can be seen in forests, where the trees grow very tall because they are competing for the light. Other organisms, such as predator and prey, are in direct conflict, as each strives to survive. Some, such as fleas, are parasites that live totally at the expense of their host. And in symbiosis, two species live together – in some cases for their mutual benefit, and in others for the benefit of only one species.

> Parasites live on or in the body of another organism. The largest is the tapeworm, which grows up to 12m (40 ft) long inside its host's intestines. A tapeworm in a whale was found to be 30m (nearly 100ft) long. A whipworm produces more than 1,000 eggs every day for 6-8 years.

Predators and prey

When predators chase their prey, it is usually the slowest prey animals that get caught. So evolution has continued to produce faster-running animals, until some sort of limit is reached (an animal's legs can only be so long). The predators are forced to evolve in a similar way, and the result is a "biological arms race". Some prey animals rely on strong defences, such as a hard shell or thick leathery skin to protect them from predators. In this sort of arms race, the predator tends to develop long stabbing teeth or powerful claws to overcome such defences.

The pheasant is a common prey of the red fox.

Parasites

Parasites are organisms that live on or in another organism (the host) and rely on it for their food. They occur among all forms of life. Microscopic disease-causing bacteria and viruses are parasites. Larger parasites include blood-sucking insects such as lice and fleas, sap-sucking aphids and weevils (insects that are parasites on plants), and worms such as tapeworms that live in the host's intestines. Parasitic plants are easy to recognize because they usually lack chlorophyll and so are not green. They get all their food from the host plant, and do not need to photosynthesize.

The parasitic dodder twines round other plants.

Give and take

When aphids feed on plant sap they get far more sugar than they need, because sap contains a lot more sugar than protein. So the aphids get rid of the excess sugar in a sticky liquid called honeydew. The aphids are helpless against predators such as ladybirds. Ants are not and can drive away many of the aphids' enemies. The aphids benefit from the ants presence so to encourage the ants, aphids store up the honeydew in their bodies and release it only when ants stroke them. This is an example of mutualism – a close relationship in which both species benefit.

Another type of relationship is commensalism, in which only one of the species benefits. But it does so without causing any harm to the other one. A common example is a small animal that feeds on the scraps left over from a larger animal's meals.

Ants collecting honeydew from black aphids

Decomposers

Feeding on dead things and biological waste products is a small army of decomposers, or saprotrophs. Without them the world would soon be knee-deep in dead matter. One important group of decomposers are moulds and fungi, most of which live in this way. Many grow on dead trees and other plant waste (such as rotten fruit). Although fungi are usually decomposers, some also grow on live trees that have been weakened in some way – in other words, they can switch from being decomposers to being parasites when the right opportunity arises. Other decomposers are dung beetles, which bury balls of dung along with their eggs to provide food for the young when they hatch. Carrion beetles do the same thing with carcasses of dead animals.

A dung beetle rolling a ball of antelope dung

Most toadstools live on decaying vegetation.

POPULATIONS

Some animals, such as fish, live in vast populations. The most populous bird ever was the North American passenger pigeon. Flocks of these birds numbered 2,000 million, and were 6.5km (4 miles) wide and 480km (300 miles) long – they took three days to fly past. All were hunted to extinction.

If you study the birds in a particular area, you will notice that there are far more of some species than others. There may be big flocks of starlings or pigeons all feeding together, quite a few finches of various kinds, but only one blackbird or robin. In general, the size of the population (the number of a given species in an area) depends on the amount of available food. But many birds and mammals establish territories and keep out others of the same species. Birds may sing or call to do this, while many mammals mark out their territory with scent produced in special glands.

Changing populations

Sizes of populations vary all the time, especially if the climate changes. During a drought, for example, some plant-eating animals cannot find enough food. As a result they rear fewer young so their populations fall. Sometimes an outbreak of a disease develops into an epidemic and greatly reduces the numbers in a population.

A few animal populations change in a regular cycle of "boom or bust". For instance in the tundra, there is a population explosion of lemmings about once every four years. Snowy owls, which prey on lemmings, follow a similar cycle as a result, laying more eggs in years of plentiful food supply. Nobody knows why some populations go in cycles whereas others do not.

The numbers of lemmings varies from year to year.

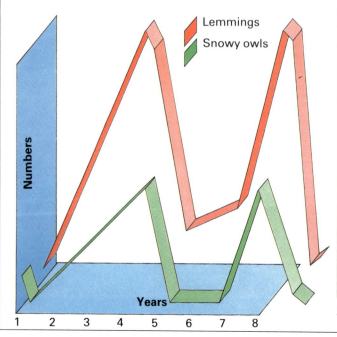

Snowy owls lay more eggs if lemmings are plentiful.

20

Territories and areas

Many birds and mammals establish and defend territories to provide enough food for themselves and their families. But it is also important in finding a mate – for many birds it is the male that holds a territory and a female will only mate with him if he has one. The fact that he can successfully defend a territory shows that he is strong and healthy, and will make a good father.

Animals claim territories in various ways. Many birds sing or call to proclaim their ownership, although some will fight for it. Blackbirds or thrushes taking turns to sing are usually neighbours reminding each other that they have a patch of land to defend. Mammals rely more on scent marking to stake their claims.

Golden pheasants defend territory by fighting.

Alone or in groups

An adult grizzly bear lives an entirely solitary life, apart from a day or two each season when it mates. By contrast, a wildebeest spends its whole life in a large herd. Between these extremes there is every degree of sociability. Some animals, such monkeys, live in family groups. Others, such as swans, form lifelong partnerships. The advantage of living in a large group, to a wildebeest or a fish such as a herring, is greater protection from predators. For other animals that live in family groups, such as wolves, the benefit is that the group helps to care for the young.

Hatchet fish find safety by swimming in shoals.

The albatross lives a mainly solitary life.

HABITATS

Tropical forests cover 10 per cent of the Earth's surface area, and boreal coniferous forests cover another 10 per cent. Desert and tundra together cover about a quarter of the total land surface, but account for only 2 per cent of the total weight of plants.

Around the North and South Poles it is too cold for any plants to grow. At the equator where the temperatures are highest, dense forest covers most of the land. In between the poles and the equator there is a gradual change in vegetation as the climate gets warmer. If things were that simple, a vegetation map of the world would just have a series of horizontal bands. But there is another important factor: rainfall. Because of the way winds blow around the globe, some regions get very little rain and have become deserts. Areas that are dry part of the year have scrub or savanna vegetation.

Some types of vegetation are found only in the Northern Hemisphere because there is no land at the corresponding latitude south of the equator.

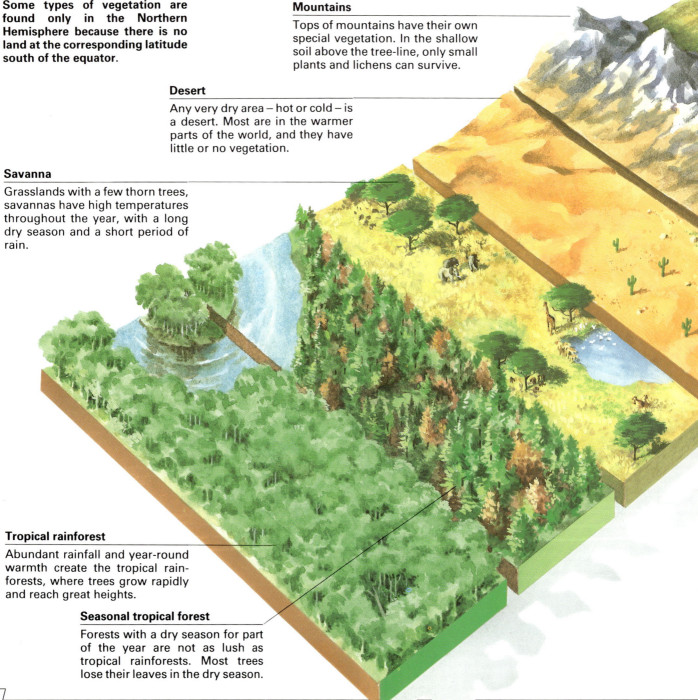

Mountains
Tops of mountains have their own special vegetation. In the shallow soil above the tree-line, only small plants and lichens can survive.

Desert
Any very dry area – hot or cold – is a desert. Most are in the warmer parts of the world, and they have little or no vegetation.

Savanna
Grasslands with a few thorn trees, savannas have high temperatures throughout the year, with a long dry season and a short period of rain.

Tropical rainforest
Abundant rainfall and year-round warmth create the tropical rainforests, where trees grow rapidly and reach great heights.

Seasonal tropical forest
Forests with a dry season for part of the year are not as lush as tropical rainforests. Most trees lose their leaves in the dry season.

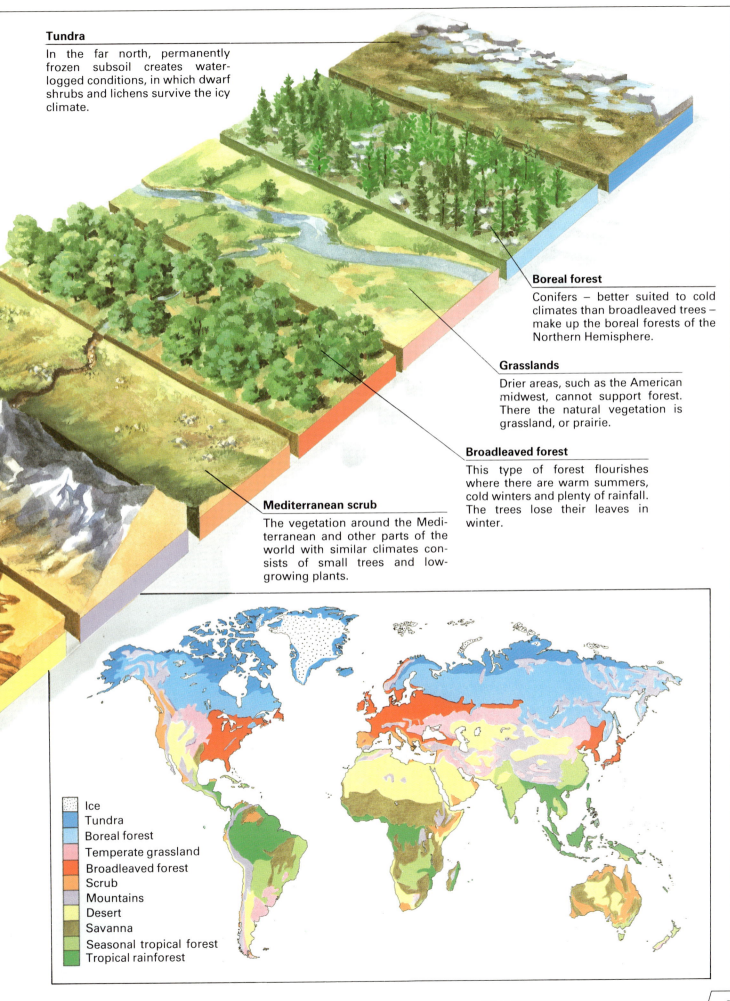

Tundra
In the far north, permanently frozen subsoil creates waterlogged conditions, in which dwarf shrubs and lichens survive the icy climate.

Boreal forest
Conifers – better suited to cold climates than broadleaved trees – make up the boreal forests of the Northern Hemisphere.

Grasslands
Drier areas, such as the American midwest, cannot support forest. There the natural vegetation is grassland, or prairie.

Broadleaved forest
This type of forest flourishes where there are warm summers, cold winters and plenty of rainfall. The trees lose their leaves in winter.

Mediterranean scrub
The vegetation around the Mediterranean and other parts of the world with similar climates consists of small trees and low-growing plants.

- Ice
- Tundra
- Boreal forest
- Temperate grassland
- Broadleaved forest
- Scrub
- Mountains
- Desert
- Savanna
- Seasonal tropical forest
- Tropical rainforest

Savanna

Savanna consists of grassland with a few scattered trees, mainly acacias, or thorn trees, which can withstand the dry season. Fire is an important factor. When everything is tinder-dry, fires start naturally, and many plants have special adaptations to survive fires and grow again.

The best-known savannas are the extensive grasslands of Africa. Many grazing animals, such as zebras and antelopes, live there and are preyed on by carnivores such as lions and leopards. As the dry season approaches, vast herds of grazers such as wildebeest migrate thousands of kilometres to find food. When the rains come and the lush new grass grows, the animals migrate back again to take advantage of the food supply.

A herd of zebras on the African savanna

Deserts

Desert regions vary widely. Most are extremely hot (at least in the daytime), but some, such as the deserts of Mongolia, are very cold. Even deserts like the Sahara are cold at night. For this reason, the plants and animals of a desert must be able to survive extremes of temperature as well as the dryness.

Most desert plants have special ways of storing water. Cacti have fat, water-filled stems and thick skins to keep water in. Desert animals are also adapted to the dry conditions. Some, such as desert frogs, remain dormant until it rains, and then they breed and lay their eggs. The tadpoles develop into adult frogs in a few weeks.

Long legs raise a lizard off hot sand.

A screech owl nests in a hole in a cactus.

Arctic and tundra

There are few plants on the land in the Arctic and Antarctic, so all the animals that live there have to get their food from the sea. Single-celled photosynthesizers in the plankton at the topmost layer of the sea produce food that larger animals, such as fish, feed on. Seals and penguins eat fish, and predators such as polar bears eat seals.

The slightly warmer lands south of the Arctic support tundra vegetation, typically lichens, mosses and dwarf shrubs. The subsoil is permanently frozen, but in the summer there are lakes and boggy pools which provide ideal breeding grounds for flying insects such as mosquitoes. They help to provide food for the birds that migrate to the tundra in their millions to nest and rear chicks. As winter approaches, they fly south again to warmer climates.

A polar bear's thick, oily fur keeps out the cold.

Scrub

Scrub is any type of vegetation with small trees, bushes and low-growing plants adapted to dry, hot summers. Mediterranean scrub is a particular type found around the Mediterranean Sea. Small areas also occur in parts of Australia and California where the climate is similar. Nearer the equator there is another kind of scrub where the savanna blends with the seasonal forest. Insects are abundant in scrubland, and many animals feed on them, particularly lizards and insectivorous birds.

Unfertile scrubland in central Greece

Mountains

Mountain plants have to survive intense cold, especially at night, and thin soil that is easily swept away by rain and wind. Mountain animals face similar problems, as well as a lack of places to shelter. Wild goats and sheep are some of the most successful. They are remarkably sure-footed and can leap from one rocky crag to another in search of plants to eat. Some predators, such as foxes and wolves, move up into the mountains in summer, but retreat to the valleys in winter.

The bighorn sheep lives in high mountains.

Swamps and marshes

In swamps and marshes the ground is permanently waterlogged. Tall reeds are a common type of vegetation, and they provide an excellent home for many small mammals and birds, and a breeding ground for millions of insects. Birds of prey, such as the marsh harrier, fly low over the reeds, seeking out small animals and swooping down among the reeds to seize them in their talons. Other predators, such as herons and otters, feed off fish and frogs that thrive in the swampy water. Ducks and geese feed mainly on plants, and make their nests in the reeds.

In the tropics, swamps provide homes for turtles, terrapins, alligators and giant snakes such as the anaconda, which glides through the shallow water in search of prey.

Horses in the swamps of Camargue, France

Seashore life

Throughout the world there is a special sort of habitat where the land meets the sea. In the Northern Hemisphere, the shoreline may be sandy or rocky, with different types of plants and animals living on each. The influence of the tides, rising and falling twice a day, is very important. The lower shore is always covered with water except at the spring tides (twice a month). In the middle intertidal zone, plants and animals are covered by the sea twice a day, while the high intertidal zone has long dry periods during low tide. Above this there is the splash zone, wetted by only the highest tides. It has its own special animals and plants.

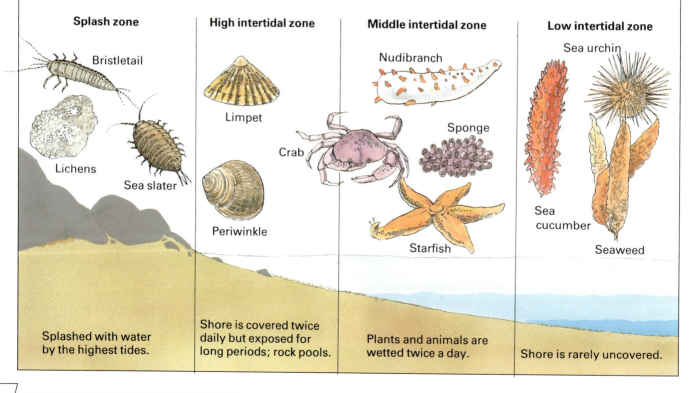

Forest and woodland

Trees are the natural vegetation of much of the Earth's land surface. Different types suit different climates, so there are several major forest zones (see map on page 23). The boreal forests of the north consist mainly of conifers, such as firs and pines, which are adapted to the harsh conditions. Snow slides off the downward slope of their branches, and their tough needles are not damaged by frost as thin leaves would be. By keeping their needles through winter, they are ready as soon as spring arrives to start photosynthesizing and to make best use of the short summer growing season. Farther south, in temperate regions, is a band of broadleaved forest. It is made up of deciduous trees such as oak and beech, which shed their leaves in autumn. The forests of the tropics are much richer in animal life, especially the tropical rainforest where there is constant growth and activity all the year round.

An ancient oak forest with moss-covered stones

Deforestation

People have been cutting down trees for thousands of years, ever since farming began in prehistoric times. Most of the deciduous forests of Europe were lost in this way. In the tropics, the rainforest had remained largely untouched until this century because the trees are so massive that they were difficult to clear before machines became available. Now even this forest is being felled and at the present rate there will soon be none left.

Destroying Amazon forest trees to make a road

Acid rain

Many forests in the Northern Hemisphere are now dying because of pollution. Gases such as sulphur dioxide released by burning coal and oil in power stations, and nitrogen oxides from car and lorry exhausts enter the atmosphere and dissolve in rain to form acids. The acid rain falls on forests and lakes, affects the soil and water and kills the trees and fish. But because the forests and lakes are habitats for many animals, they too are affected and die.

German forest trees killed by acid rain

CONSERVATION

The biggest effect on the environment is caused by the growth of the human race. In the last hundred years, the world's population has increased from 1,500 million to 5,000 million. At the current rate of growth, by the year 2000 it will be about 6,000 million and will begin to stabilize at about twice that figure by the 22nd century.

Ten thousand years ago, human beings lived by hunting and by gathering berries and nuts. Like other living things, they were part of a complicated food web, and their population remained fairly constant. Then people began farming and everything changed. People altered the ecosystem so that the food web produced more and more of the sort of food they could eat. The human population began to rise, and other animals were squeezed out.

In the present century this process has accelerated rapidly. World population is growing faster than ever. Scientists produce pesticides, which kill many living things (not just pests). Other chemicals pollute the soil, the rivers, seas and air – posing another major threat to life. Many biologists believe that the world could be approaching a major environmental crisis.

Preserving the habitat

There are now very few untouched natural habitats, such as coral reefs and tropical rainforests. It is important to preserve these areas because they provide a home for many animals and plants that cannot survive anywhere else. And once the habitats are destroyed, they cannot usually be recreated.

Even where there is farming, forestry or other human activity on the land, it is still possible for wildlife to survive. Traditional methods of farming tended to be better than modern ones, because the land was not used so intensively – there was still room for wild plants and animals. Returning to less intensive methods and reducing the use of pesticides would result in more wildlife.

Coral reefs are in danger from fishermen.

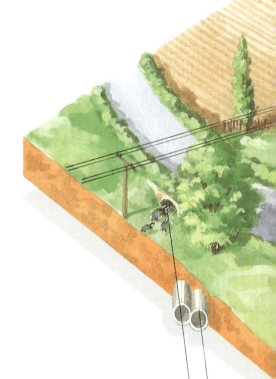

Under-road badger passage
Many animals are killed by road vehicles. Badgers and toads, which regularly cross roads at a particular place, can be helped by underpasses.

Oil pipelines
The natural appearance of the environment can be preserved by laying oil and gas pipelines, and electricity cables, underground.

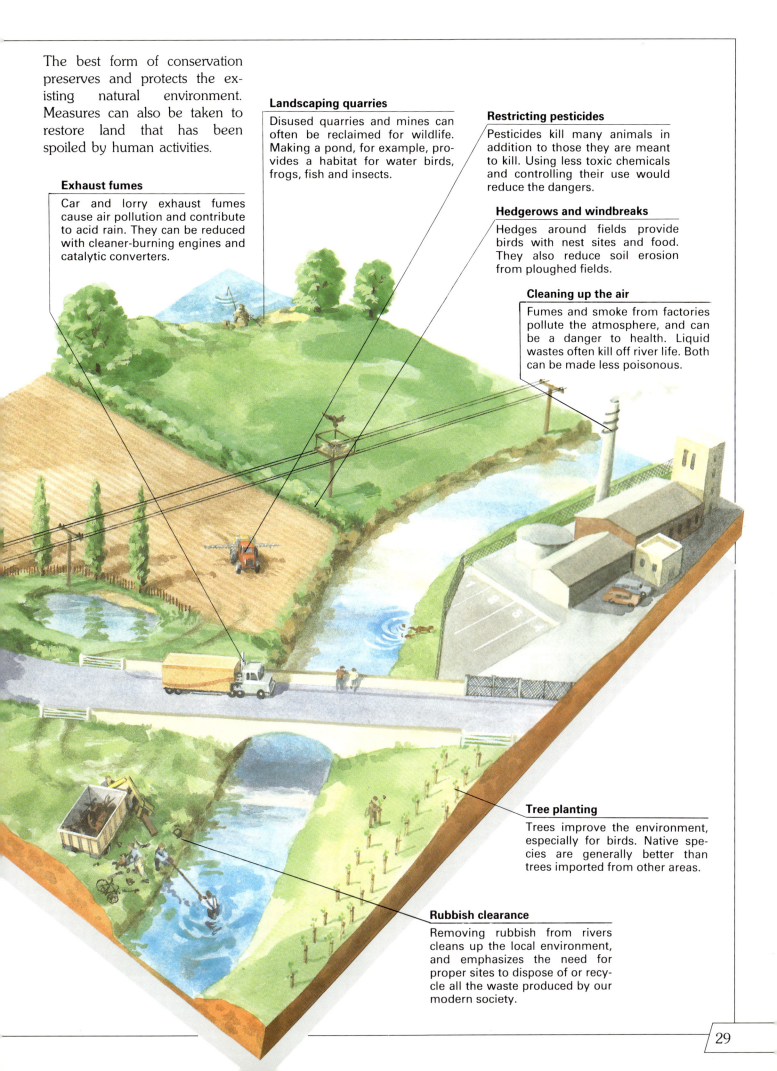

The best form of conservation preserves and protects the existing natural environment. Measures can also be taken to restore land that has been spoiled by human activities.

Exhaust fumes
Car and lorry exhaust fumes cause air pollution and contribute to acid rain. They can be reduced with cleaner-burning engines and catalytic converters.

Landscaping quarries
Disused quarries and mines can often be reclaimed for wildlife. Making a pond, for example, provides a habitat for water birds, frogs, fish and insects.

Restricting pesticides
Pesticides kill many animals in addition to those they are meant to kill. Using less toxic chemicals and controlling their use would reduce the dangers.

Hedgerows and windbreaks
Hedges around fields provide birds with nest sites and food. They also reduce soil erosion from ploughed fields.

Cleaning up the air
Fumes and smoke from factories pollute the atmosphere, and can be a danger to health. Liquid wastes often kill off river life. Both can be made less poisonous.

Tree planting
Trees improve the environment, especially for birds. Native species are generally better than trees imported from other areas.

Rubbish clearance
Removing rubbish from rivers cleans up the local environment, and emphasizes the need for proper sites to dispose of or recycle all the waste produced by our modern society.

ENDANGERED SPECIES

More than 90 per cent of all species that have ever lived have become extinct, mostly because of natural – rather than human – causes. But the rate of extinction is higher now than at any time in the Earth's history. Figures may be as high as one species of plant or animal every day.

Many plants and animals are now in danger of dying out altogether. Most of these endangered species are becoming extinct because their habitats are being destroyed. Some, such as the large whales, are threatened because of over-hunting. Often it is a combination of the two. Chimpanzees are in danger because the forests in which they live are being cut down. But the situation is made worse by hunters, who kill the adults and capture the young ones for use in medical research. Studies on the Aids virus now being done have further increased the demand for these animals.

Profiting from wildlife

Many natural objects are very beautiful, and people have always used things such as feathers, shells and animal skins for decoration. But when people begin selling such objects they have to obtain large quantities of them to meet the demand and make a profit. This can often result in the wholesale destruction of a wild species. Many coral reefs have been badly damaged by ships towing iron bars over them to break them up – the pieces are sold to tourists as souvenirs. When the coral goes, so do all the unique animals that live on the reef. Some animals hunted for their skins are now endangered, and so are many others that are collected for the trade in pets. Terrapins are trapped in their thousands in some parts of the world. Most die in transit, and only a few of those collected survive to become pets.

Terrapins are threatened by the trade in pets.

Jaguar furs confiscated by Brazilian authorities

Too few to survive

One of the dangers facing wild animals as their numbers decline is that the population may become too low to survive. Normally animals do not mate with close relatives. But if the numbers fall low enough they may have to. Mating with close relatives (inbreeding) tends to produce weaker young, so the population declines even further. The same problem occurs when a habitat becomes fragmented, so that the population forms small isolated groups that cannot therefore interbreed. This is what has happened to the Giant panda in China. Pandas feed on bamboo, but the bamboo forests have been reduced to small pockets – and the animals will not cross the open land between them. The Chinese are now planting corridors of bamboo linking some of the fragments. Moving animals from one area to another to avoid inbreeding can also help.

The purple orchid is a protected plant.

Game wardens with a baby Sumatran rhinoceros

Island life

Some islands far out in the ocean were produced by undersea volcanoes, so they began with no life at all. Gradually they were colonized by a few plants and animals – carried by the wind or on natural rafts. They then often evolved in unusual ways, resulting in unique species. Many birds became flightless. But they were easy prey for humans and animals they took with them, such as cats, dogs and rats. As a result, many island species have become extinct.

Marine iguanas are unique to the Galapagos Islands.

The takahe is a rare New Zealand rail.

PRESERVING WILDLIFE

Every year, 12 million hectares (30 million acres) of forest are cut down – an area almost as big as England. A similar area is severely damaged. Along the U.S. coast alone, 20,000 sq km (7,800 sq miles) of wetlands, valuable habitats for birds, have been drained or filled in and converted to arable land.

Preventing species from becoming extinct is a difficult but important task. One of the successful rescue missions is Project Tiger in India, which has rescued the tiger by setting up huge reserves. Such reserves are valuable because they also benefit other wildlife, especially smaller animals such as insects, which do not cause as much public concern as tigers and other large mammals. All the plants and animals in an ecosystem, however small, are important in preserving its natural balance. The loss of one species in a food chain can lead to survival problems for another.

Zoos

Zoos can have an important part to play in preserving endangered species, but not everyone agrees that they are a good thing. They are valuable in breeding animals that are very scarce in the wild and building up their populations. Animals bred in captivity can then be released to increase the numbers in the wild. The difficulty is to keep wild animals in conditions that allow them to lead full, natural lives. Some studies have revealed that many zoo animals do not survive well because of captivity. And zoos cost a lot of money to run. They therefore have to earn money by "entertaining" the public, which is not always in the best interests of the animals.

Soon the only giant pandas may be those in zoos.

Botanical gardens

Botanical gardens are places where plants from throughout the world are grown so that they can be studied and compared by botanists. By using greenhouses where the temperature and moisture content of the air (humidity) are carefully regulated, such gardens can grow plants from many different climates – from deserts to tropical rainforests. Like zoos, they can have an important role to play in preserving species that are endangered in the wild. Some of these may be useful to humankind in breeding better crop plants. Many wild plants are resistant to insects, for example, and a plant breeder can transfer this characteristic to a related crop plant.

Amazonian water lilies at Kew Gardens in London.

Preserving the habitat

There is little point in saving a species from extinction merely to preserve it as a living specimen in a botanical garden or a zoo. It is much more important to save the habitat in which it lives. A major threat to habitats in the tropics is the growth of human populations. With more and more people needing a plot of land on which to grow food, more of the tropical forest trees are being chopped down. But often the land proves to be useless once the trees have gone – the soil is poor and easily washed away by heavy rain. This is happening in much of the Amazon basin, in Indonesia and in Madagascar.

One way of preserving the natural habitat is the establishment of National Parks. In many cases the survival of rare species has been made possible because a National Park has been created for them. These areas also offer invaluable opportunities for studying organisms in their environment.

Forests in Madagascar are burned to make land suitable for agriculture.

The Painted Desert National Park in Arizona, USA.

Breeding in captivity

By 1972, the Arabian oryx had been hunted to extinction in the wild. But ten years earlier conservationists had realized the danger and had established a captive herd. When the herd had grown large enough, some of the animals were released into a desert reserve in Oman – to re-establish the wild population. This was a success, and shows how useful captive breeding can be as long as the animals' natural habitat still exists. A similar programme in Britain is releasing captive-bred otters into areas with a suitable habitat. One difficulty with such schemes is to breed the animals in captivity without making them too tame and unafraid of human beings.

The rare Arabian oryx was bred in captivity.

EXTINCTION CHART

Extinction is a necessary part of evolution – it has been happening since life on Earth began. But today it is people who are responsible for most extinctions, and the rate has accelerated enormously during this century. Most has been caused by hunting and the destruction of habitats. Many mammals and birds have disappeared, and a great many more are endangered. There are also a large number of reptiles, amphibians and fish – and thousands of species of plants and insects – that die out every year. The tropical rainforests are a major area of loss, partly because it has such a tremendous variety of wildlife and partly because it is being destroyed at such a fast rate.

Humpback whales are in danger of extinction.

1 Mammoth
2 Woolly rhinoceros
3 Cave lion
4 Cave bear
5 Irish elk
6 American mastodon
7 Imperial mammoth
8 Great ground sloth
9 Sabre-tooth tiger
10 Dire wolf
11 Reunion solitaire
12 Dodo
13 Guadaloupe amazon
14 Elephant bird
15 Aurochs
16 Steller's sea cow
17 Blue buck
18 Hispaniolan hutia
19 Green-and-yellow macaw
20 Moa
21 Dwarf emu
22 Rodriguez little owl
23 Sandwich rail
24 Great auk
25 Spectacled cormorant
26 Atlas bear
27 Tarpan
28 Sea mink
29 Portuguese ibex
30 Quagga
31 Warrah
32 Palestine painted frog
33 Abingdon Island tortoise
34 Round Island boa
35 Passenger pigeon
36 Carolina parakeet
37 Pink-headed duck
38 Lord Howe Island white-eye
39 Hawaiian O-O
40 Madagascar serpent eagle
41 Kauai Nukupuu
42 Greater rabbit bandicoot
43 Arizona jaguar
44 Schomburgk's deer
45 Caribbean monk seal
46 Thylacine
47 Jamaican long-tongued bat
48 Barbary lion
49 Newfoundland white wolf
50 Bali tiger
51 Italian spade-footed toad
52 Chinese alligator
53 Central Asian cobra
54 Geometric tortoise
55 Hawksbill turtle
56 Japanese crested ibis
57 California condor
58 Red-billed curassow
59 Black robin
60 Reunion petrel
61 Abbott's booby
62 Hawaiian gallinule
63 Mauritius pink pigeon
64 Western ground parrot
65 Hawaiian crow
66 Leadbeater's opossum
67 Ghost bat
68 Woolly spider monkey
69 Mountain gorilla
70 Blue whale
71 Humpback whale
72 Indus dolphin
73 Northern kit fox
74 Baluchistan bear
75 Giant otter
76 Siberian tiger
77 Asiatic lion
78 Mediterranean monk seal
79 Grevy's zebra
80 Przewalski's horse
81 Mountain tapir
82 Great Indian rhinoceros
83 Swamp deer
84 Giant sable antelope
85 Indri
86 Orangutan
87 Sumatran rhinoceros
88 Mountain anoa

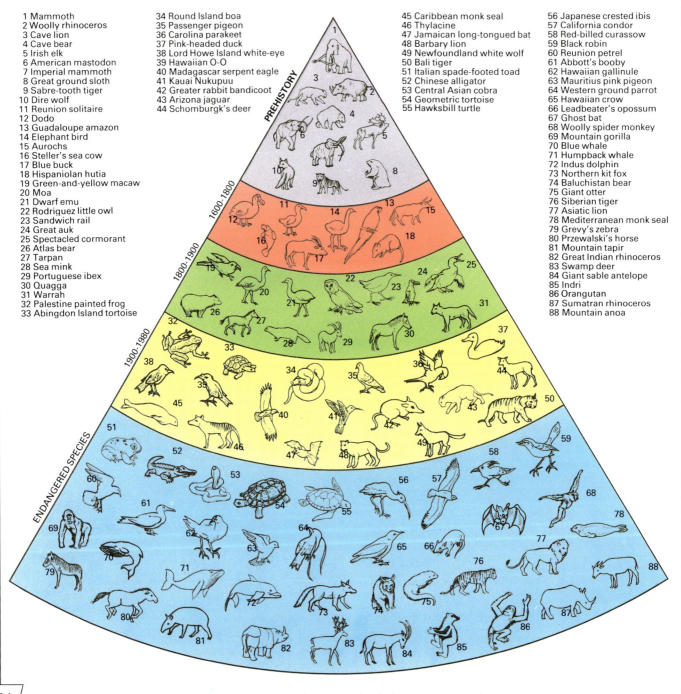

GLOSSARY

autotrophs organisms that make their own food using simple starting materials such as water and carbon dioxide gas. They need a source of energy, and most use sunlight, in a process called photosynthesis. A few bacteria can use chemical energy stored in simple chemical compounds such as hydrogen sulphide.

biodegradable describing a substance that can be broken down by bacteria, fungi and other living organisms (decomposers). All materials produced by living things are biodegradable, but most synthetic materials, such as plastics, are not.

biome distinctive type of ecosystem that occurs over a wide area. Rainforest, mangrove swamp and coniferous forest are good examples. A biome is sometimes called an 'environment' or 'habitat'.

calorie unit of measurement used for heat energy or energy in foods.

carbon dioxide gas found in the Earth's atmosphere. It is used by plants to make food: they combine several molecules of carbon dioxide with water to make a molecule of sugar. Carbon dioxide is produced when plants and animals break down food to yield energy.

carnivores animals that eat other animals.

commensalism close relationship between two species in which one benefits, and the other neither gains nor loses; a form of symbiosis.

community all the living organisms within a particular area.

decomposers organisms that feed on the remains of living things, or on the waste products they produce (e.g. cow dung). In feeding on these items, decomposers provide a valuable service in removing them and in returning the nutrients they contain to the soil or water. The major decomposers are bacteria and fungi, but other animals can act as decomposers, including dung beetles and vultures.

ecosystem all the living organisms in a particular region, as well as the soil, water and other non-living features that interact with them.

environment the conditions in which an organism lives. *See also* biome.

extinction the complete dying out of a species.

habitat particular ecosystem in which a given organism lives. *See also* biome.

herbivores animals that eat plants.

heterotrophs organisms that cannot make their own food (as autotrophs can). They have to eat other living things to get energy. All animals and fungi are heterotrophs, and so are many bacteria.

insectivores animals that eat insects.

mutualism close relationship between two different species in which both benefit; a form of symbiosis.

nitrates chemical compounds that contain nitrogen and oxygen. They are found naturally in the soil, and plants use them to make protein molecules – proteins contain nitrogen, and the nitrates act as a source of this element. Farmers add nitrates to the soil in the form of fertilizer to increase the yields of crop plants.

nutrients substances that are needed by an animal, plant or other living organism in order to stay alive.

oxygen gas that makes up 20 per cent of the Earth's atmosphere. Most living organisms cannot live without oxygen, and use it to break down food and release energy from it.

pesticides chemicals used to kill off unwanted organisms. They include insecticides (which kill insects), fungicides (which kill fungi, mostly fungal diseases of plants such as mildew and rust) and herbicides (which kill weeds).

photosynthesis using sunlight to make food. It is practised by plants, algae, cyanobacteria and some other bacteria.

pollution release of unwanted or dangerous materials into the natural environment. Some pollution is caused by natural forces, such as volcanoes that throw out ash and lava. But most pollution results from human activities, such as the spraying of crops with pesticides.

population all the members of a given species of plants or animals that live within a particular area. The members of a population can interbreed freely, so there is an unrestricted flow of genes within the population.

soil erosion loss of soil from the land. It can be washed away by rain or rivers, or blown away by the wind. Soil erosion is often the result of bad farming practices: the roots of plants normally bind the soil and prevent erosion. Removing plant cover by over-grazing with animals, felling forests or destroying hedges and other windbreaks, can result in erosion.

symbiosis close relationship between two different organisms. There are several forms of symbiosis, including mutualism and commensalism. (Some scientists use symbiosis in a different way, to mean just relationships in which both species benefit).

INDEX

All entries in bold are found in the Glossary

acid rain 27
air 3, 4, 8
algae 5
amphibians 5
ants 19
aphids 18, 19
Arabian oryx 33

bacteria 4-6, 8-9, 10, 16, 18
badgers 16
bats 7
bears 16, 21, 25
biological clock 13
biomass 16
biomes 14, 16, **35**
birds 5, 7, 12, 13, 17, 20, 21, 25, 26, 31
blood 8, 13
bones 4, 8
boreal forests 22, 23, 27
botanical gardens 32
broadleaved woodland 14, 23, 27

cacti 24
cactus wren 14-15
calcium 8
camels 8
captive breeding 33
carbon dioxide 6, 8, 9, **35**
carnivores (meat-eaters) 6-7, 14, 16, 17, 24, **35**
cell division 10, 11
cells 4, 7, 8, 10-11
cellulose 6, 9, 10
chlorophyll 6, 18
chloroplasts 6
chromosomes 10
commensalism 19, **35**
communication 13
communities 14-15, **35**
conifers 5, 27
conservation 28-34
coral reef 14, 28, 30
crabs 8, 11
crustaceans 11

decomposers 5, 14, 16, 19, **35**

deforestation 27
desert 14, 16, 22, 24
DNA 10
dung beetles 19

ecologists 16, 28
ecosystems 14, 16, 28, 32, **35**
eggs 7, 11, 17, 20
elephants 6, 7
energy 6-7, 8, 10, 16
environment 3, 28-34, **35**
evolution 14, 18
exoskeletons 11
extinction 3, 14, 20, 27, 30-34, **35**

fire 24
fish 5, 8, 13, 17, 20, 21, 25, 26
fleas 18
food 4-5, 6-7, 9-10, 13, 16-18, 20-21, 24-25, 28
food chains 16-17, 32
food webs 16-17, 28
forests 16, 18, 27, 32
foxes 16-17, 18, 25
fruits 7, 9
fungi 4, 5, 6, 16, 19

giant panda 31
giant worms 9
grass 5, 16, 24
grasslands 23, 24
growth 4, 6, 7, 10-11

habitats 20, 22-28, 31-33
herbivores (plant-eaters) 6-7, 14, 16, 20
honeydew 19
hormones 12
humans 3, 4, 13, 17, 28, 30
hydrothermal vents 9

inbreeding 31
information 12-13
insects 4, 5, 6, 7, 11, 14, 18, 25, 26, 32
ivy-leaved toadflax 12

leaves 6, 7
lemmings 20
lice 18
lichens 17
lions 7, 24
lizards 24, 25
lungs 4, 8

mammals 5, 10, 11, 20, 21, 26, 32
marshes 26
membrane 10
microscopic organisms 4, 5, 8, 18
minerals 8, 9, 11
monkeys 7, 21
mosquitoes 25
mosses 5
moulds 19
mountains 22, 25
muscles 4, 7
mutualism 19, **35**

National Parks 33
nitrates 8, 16, **35**
non-living things 4, 5, 14
nutrients 8, 16, **35**

oceans 8, 9, 25
omnivores 7, 16
otters 17, 26, 33
oxygen 3, 4, 6, 8, **35**

parasites 4, 18, 19
pesticides 17, 28, **35**
pheromones 13
phosphates 8
photosynthesis 5, 6, 7, 9, 18, 25, 27, **35**
phytoplankton 8, 13
pineal gland 12
plankton 25
pollination 14
pollution 17, 27, 28, **35**
population 20-21, 28, 30, **35**
predators 17-19, 21, 25, 26
prey 17, 18, 19
Project Tiger 32

proteins 9, 10, 19
protoplasm 10

rabbits 16-17
rainfall 22, 24
reproduction 4, 6

sap 9, 18, 19
saprotrophs 19
savanna 22, 24, 25
scents 13, 20, 21
scrub 22, 23, 25
seashores 26
seeds 9, 13, 14
senses 12-13
skeleton 4, 11
smells 13
snakes 7, 15
sociability 21
soil 3, 4, 5, 8, 9, 14, 15, 16, 25, 33, **35**
starch 6, 9
stomata 8
sugars 6, 9, 19
sunlight 6, 8, 12, 18
swamps 26
symbiosis 18, **35**

territory 20-21
tides 26
trace elements 8
trees 3, 4, 5, 7, 8, 18-19, 24, 27
tropical rainforest 14, 16, 22, 27, 28, 33, 34
tundra 20, 22, 23, 25

viruses 4, 18

water 3-6, 8-10, 14, 24
wildebeest 21, 24
wolves 16, 21, 25
worms 4, 5, 18

yucca moth 14-15
yucca trees 14-15
yucca weevil 14-15

zoos 32

Photographic Credits
Cover and pages 19 (right), 21 (right), 25 (top) and 27 (left): Zefa; intro page and pages 7 (both), 9, 11, 13 (top), 20 (bottom), 21 (top), 24 (top and left), 25 (right), 26, 27 (top), 31 (bottom left), 33 (middle) and 34: Planet Earth/Seaphot; pages 6, 8 (left), 10, 13 (left and right), 17 (left), 18 (both), 19 (top), 20 (top), 21 (top), 24 (right), 25 (left), 27 (right), 28, 30 (right), 31 (top left, top right and bottom right) and 33 (bottom): Bruce Coleman; pages 8 (right) and 32 (left and right): Robert Harding Library; page 12 (bottom): L. Gamlin; page 17 (right): Hutchison Library; page 30 (left): Survival; page 33 (top): Ardea; back cover: Planet Earth.